MACHINES ON THE MOVE

TRAINS

by Natalie Deniston

TABLE OF CONTENTS

Tadpole Books, an imprint of Jump! Library by FlutterBee

WORDS TO KNOW

cars

engine

pulls

ride

station

tracks

TRAINS

A train goes by.

It moves on tracks.

It has an engine.

car

It pulls cars.

This one goes fast.

EMERGENCY EXIT

We ride.

2

It stops at the station.

LET'S REVIEW!

Trains carry people and goods from place to place. What color is this train's engine?

INDEX